This book is dedicated to all the readers of Chitra Banerjee Divakaruni.

FROM SHADOWS TO ROOTS: PARENTAL RELATIONSHIPS IN OLEANDER GIRL AND QUEEN OF DREAMS

WITH REFERENCE TO CHITRA BANERJEE DIVAKARUNI'S 'KAROBI AND RAKHI'

DR. R SUDHA

Made with ♥ on the Notion Press Platform
www.notionpress.com

Contents

Foreword

The book entitled "From Shadows to Roots: Parental Relationships in *Oleander Girl* and *Queen of Dreams*" deals with the protagonists Karobi and Rakhi who strive hard to unveil the mystery in their parental figures. Karobi goes through a change in her personality both mentally and physically and faces many challenges in her journey of life. True to her name, Karobi, which means 'oleander', she

is beautiful and also stubborn. Her journey to find her father in America, and her determination to face obstacles make her reach the truth she is in search of. Her way of handling the crises of her life, her resistance to cross-cultural and other temptations and the strong urge to follow her heart irrespective of the reactions of the people around her define her individuality. Rakhi, in the novel *Queen of Dreams*, strongly emphasizes the significance of familial ties and roots. As an immigrant's daughter, facing many odds, the protagonist in the novel puts much effort unravelling the history behind her mother who is an Indian and a dream- teller. Her mental trauma fills her with the urge to know her true roots and family heritage of her Indian mother, thus setting her on a venture of discovery. The novel depicts her successful journey and the way she holds the relationships together to rediscover her roots.

Dr. M Divya

Assistant Professor of English

Preface

From Shadows to Roots: Parental Relationships in *Oleander Girl* and *Queen of Dreams* deals with the protogonists Karobi and Rakhi who strive hard to unveil the mystery in their parental figures. Karobi goes through a change in her personality both mentally and physically and faces many challenges in her journey of life. True to her name, Karobi, which is named after an oleander, she is beautiful and also stubborn. Her journey to find her father in America, and her determination to face obstacles make her to reach the truth she is in search of. Her way of handling the crises of her life, her resistance to cross- cultural and other temptations and strong urge to follow her heart irrespective of the reaction of people around her define her individuality. Rakhi, in the novel *Queen of Dreams* strongly emphasizes the significance of familial ties and roots. As an immigrant's daughter, facing many odds, the protagonist in the novel displays many efforts into unravelling the history behind her mother who is an Indian and a dream- teller. Her mental trauma fills her with the urge to know her true roots and family heritage of her Indian mother, thus setting her on a venture of discovery. The novel depicts her successful journey and the way she holds the relationships together to rediscover her roots.

Preface

Acknowledgements

I express my sincere gratitude to the Almighty who bestowed His bleassing in the course of this work. I also extend my whole hearted thanks to my editor and good friend Dr. M Divya for her fruitful contribution.

Prologue

While reading Divakaruni's fiction, a reader happens to continuously move between two entirely different socio-cultural environments and comes to know several aspects of the lives of the women of both worlds. It becomes essential to have a glance at the writing of the author who vividly writes about the immigrant women, the general facets of hardships in the context of women and their relationships with their counterparts.

CHAPTER ONE

From Shadows to Roots: Parental Relationships in *Oleander Girl* and *Queen of Dreams*

Chitra Banerjee Divakaruni, a Bengali writer, belonging to the post-independent group of Indian writers is worth noted as a writer in English. Divakaruni has established herself as a distinct, versatile and extraordinary South Asian woman writer. She is one of those writers who has spent much of her life outside her native country, India and lived in the United States of America. A part of her writing is autobiographical in nature as it deals with herpersonal experiences in India and America as well. Her works primarily deal with theexperiences of women and their relationship with others around them.

Chitra Banerjee was born in Calcutta on 29th July 1956. She grew up at New Alipore in Calcutta, and spent the first nineteen years of her life in India. Her father Rajendra Kumar Banerjee was an accountant by profession and her mother Tatini Banerjee was a school teacher. Chitra was the only girl child among the four children. She was the second child to them and the other three brothers were Partha, Dhruva and Surya.

Divakaruni studied at Loreto House, a convent school run by Irish nuns. She earned her Bachelor's Degree in English from Presidency College, University of Calcutta in 1976 and in the same year she left Calcutta and moved for America. She acquired her Masters Degree in English from the Wright State University in Dayton, Ohio in 1978, and continued higher education at the age of 19. She lived in Chicago and Ohio before she settled in Sunnydale, California in 1979. She received Ph. D. in English from the University of California at Berkeley, while working under Stephen Greenbalt on the topic For Danger is in Words: A Study of Language in Marlowe's Plays in 1984. Divakaruni through different jobs paid for her education by taking babysitting, selling merchandise in an Indian boutique, slicing bread at a bakery and washing instruments at a science lab so on.

Divakaruni was interested in the issues involving women. She worked with Afghani women refugees and the troubled Indian women in America. She became the founder member and President of the organization MAITRI in 1991. MAITRI is an organization in San Francisco working for the South Asian women who dwell in worsen conditions. It helps women who experience domestic violence, emotional abuse and cultural alienation. It works with other social organizations to raise awareness about domestic violences of various kinds. Divakaruni's association with the organizations like MAITRI influences her writing too. The women she came across while working with these organizations found their expressions in her literary works.

Divakaruni currently serves on the advisory board of Daya, a Huston based non- profit organization that works to prevent violence against women. It helps to strengthen and promote healthy family relationship of the women of South Asian community. She has also worked for PRATHAM, a worldwide non-profitable organization, dedicated to removing illiteracy in India. PRATHAM mainly works amidst urban slums, rural outposts and prison's labour sites where children are employed. Its mission is: 'Every Child in School and Learning Well.' She admits her affinity with these social organizations and acknowledges that it influences her writing. It made her to think a lot more about the issues she was witnessing and how it related to the lives of the immigrants, and she wanted to write about it.

Her interest in women began after she left India and at this point she came to re-evaluate the treatment of women there. With the intention of uniting people, she blends together myth, mystery and the everyday reality of life which includes the various dimensions of relationships. Much of her writing moves around the immigrant women and their experiences in the settled country. Divakaruni was a well-received poet before she established herself as a novelist.

Divakaruni is a well- received poet before she established herself as a novelist. She has written poems on variety of themes. She has four volumes of poetry to her credit. *Dark Like the River*, (1987) *The Reason for Nasturtiums* (1990), and *Black Candle* (1991) are three of them. *Leaving Yuba City* (1997) is Divakaruni's fourth volume of poetry. The core area of her interest lies in the immigrant women and their troubled lives in her poetry as well.

Divakaruni has published in more than fifty magazines which include Atlantic Monthly and New Yorker. Her writing has been included in several Asian American anthologies such as *Best American Short Stories* and *The Pushcart Prize Anthology*. Her works have been translated into eleven languages including Dutch, Hebrew, Portuguese, Danish, German and Japanese.

Her collection of short stories *Arranged Marriage* won a Critical Acclaim, 1996 American Book Award, Bay Area Book Reviewers Award and the PEN Josephine Miles Award for Fiction. *The Mistress of Spices* was on several Best Books lists, including the San Francisco Chronicle's 100 Best Books of the 20th Century. *The Conch Bearer* was included in Best Books of 2003 by *Publishers Weekly*. *The Lives of Strangers* was included in O'Henry Prize Stories, 2003. *The Vine of Desire* was included in Best Books of 2002 by *Los Angeles Times and San Francisco Chronicle*. *Mrs Dutta Writes a Letter* was included in *Best American Short Stories* in 1999. *The Mistress of Spices* was included in *Best Paperbacks of* 1998, *Seattle Times* and in *Best Books of* 1997, 'Los Angeles Times'. For *Black Candle* she received Honourable Mention, Paterson Poetry Prize in 1992.

She also has received California Arts Council Award, in 1998, C.Y. Lee Creative Writing Award (1995), Allen Ginsberg Poetry Prize (1994), Pushcart Prize (1994), Pen Syndicated Fiction Awards (1993 and 1994), Gerbode Foundation Award, California (1992), Santa Clara Arts Council Award California (1990 and 1994), Editor's Choice Award by Cream City Review (1990), Barbara Deming Memorial Award, New York (1989), The Hackney Literary Award, Birmingham-Southern College Alabama (1988) and Cultural Jewel Award by Indian Culture Centre Houston(2009). She received the Pushcart Prize (2003), International House Alumna of the year award by University of California at Berkeley (2008) and South Asian Literary Association Distinguished Author Award (2007).

Divakaruni has bagged several prestigious awards such as National Book Award and the PEN Faulkner Award. Two of her books, The Mistress of Spices and Sister of My Heart, have been adopted into movies by filmmakers Gurinder Chaddha and Paul Berges (an English film) and Suhasini Mani Ratnam (a Tamil TV serial) respectively. In this way, Divakaruni has been rightly described as an award-winning author of great calibre who has dealt with the troubled lives of immigrant women from feministic stand point. Through her works of art, she has projected the hollowness of women's dream, pain, suffering, and the horrors of their lives.

Divakaruni started writing to explore the immigrant feminine experiences she encountered. Her first book of poetry *Dark Like the River* appeared in 1987. It established her as an eminent poet. In the year 1990, she published the collection of verse *The Reason for Nasturtiums*. This volume shows her interest for the immigrant experience and south Asian women who try to find their own identities in a new socio-cultural environment.

Black Candle (1991) is an earlier collection of poetry that records significant moments in the lives of the South Asian women.*Two Women outside Circus, Restroom* and *Bengal Night* are the other poems of the collection. *Leaving Yuba City: New and Selected Poems* appeared in 1997. It includes new poems as well as old ones from *Dark Like River, The Reason for Nasturtiums* and *Black Candle*. The poems are about women from India, Pakistan and Bangladesh. Themes of these poems are very similar to the subject matter of her novels, i.e., women's problems, family life, exile, alienation, exoticism, ethnicity, domesticity, love and romance.

Divakaruni's first collection of short stories *Arranged Marriage* (1995) mainly focuses on Indian immigrant women, caught between two worlds. The characters are both liberated and trapped by the cultural changes and all the struggle to find their identities. These stories explore the cross-cultural identities of women from relationship perspective. Divakaruni has created contradictory as well as connected fictional worlds through her stories in *Arranged Marriage*. How difficult it is for an Indian woman to break the shackles of her unhappy marriage with which she is trapped by the traditional Indian institute of arranged marriage is discussed in the opening story *Bats*. In *Clothes*, the narrator Sumita's husband dies and she is forced to decide whether to stay in America or return to India. In *Silver Pavements Golden Roofs*, the protagonist is a graduate, newly arrived in America considers the country as a land of illusion. However, she has to face racism on the wide Chicago road. In *Affair*, two temperamentally mismatched couples are shown divorced after a few years. Their marriage would have been arranged traditionally, based on their horoscopes having matched perfectly. In *Doors*, the character Preeti likes the western idea of privacy and does not like when her husband's friend comes to live with them.

Thus the common theme that runs through all the stories is the struggling of Indian immigrant women who strive to adjust and to find their identity for themselves through Relationships in society. The characters of the stories look varied but the theme remains the same.

Divakaruni's first novel *The Mistress of Spices* (1997) is written with a blend of mystery and reality. The chapters of the novel are named after the spices such as Cinnamon, Turmeric,Fenugreek and so on. Unlike *The Mistress of Spices*, the second novel *Sister of My Heart* (1999) is written in a realistic mode. It describes the complicated sibling relationship in a Bengali family. As the title of the novel indicates, it is the story of two sisters, their sorrows, happiness, difficulties, understanding, love, sympathy and affection for each other. Divakaruni portrays the sibling relationship with keen observations and minute details of the lives of the protagonists.

The Unknown Errors of Our Lives (2001) is a collection of short stories set in India and America. The collection includes nine stories, and eight of them have female protagonists. These are the women caught between the beliefs and traditions of their biological home and that of their adopted home. It shows the struggle of the women to be accommodated in difficult conditions and to be assimilated in different socio-cultural environment who search for their selves.

In *Mrs Dutta Writes a Letter*, a widow stays with her only son which makes her realize the tension that arises between them. The relationship between the mother and the daughter in-law is dominantly portrayed in the story by Chitra Banerjee. Miscommunication and growing distance are the central theme of *The Intelligence of Wild Things*. Ruchira, the protagonist of the title story *The Unknown Errors of Our Lives*, discovers her childhood *Book of Errors*, while she packs things up for her forthcoming marriage.

The Names of Stars in Bengali is the frank story of a San Francisco wife and mother, who returns to her native village in India to visit her mother, but is desperate to get out of India due to her restrictive existence. In this story, the author explores the theme of mother-daughter relationship. All the stories including *The Unknown Errors of our Lives* are about the lack of communication, unarticulated love and redemptive memories. They explore the difficult process of adjustment. This is an extraordinary collection of short stories that draw pain, loss and alienation of women characters due to the breach in relationships.

The novel *The Vine of Desire* appeared in 2002, when Divakaruni moved to Texas, where she taught creative writing program at the University of Houston. It is a sequel to the former novel *Sister of My Heart*. In *The Vine of Desire*, the two cousins, Anju and Sudha are reunited in America in the free culture, which is in total contrast with traditional Indian culture where women are restricted, marginalized and deprived.

Neela: Victory Song (2002) is Chitra Divakaruni's first book for children. It is a part of *Girls of Many Lands* series. Divakaruni manages to handle two different goals in this novel. One is to presentthe struggle for Indian independence, and another is how a twelve-year sensitive girl might have seen it. *The Conch Bearer* (2003) is Divakaruni's second book for children; a quest fantasy which blends action, adventure and magic. This is Divakaruni's special creation in her unique style.

Queen of Dreams (2004) is Divakaruni's sixth novel that again displays magic. In *The Mistress of Spices*, Tilo gives spices to help her customers and to solve their problems whereas in *Queen of Dreams* Mrs. Gupta deciphers the dream of others and helps them in their lives. Mrs. Gupta's daughter Rakhi is a young artist and a divorced mother living in Berkeley, California and is fascinated by her mother's ability to foresee and guide people through their fates. Rakhi feels isolated from her mother's past in India and the dream world she inhabits. She is determined to know the other side of her existence i.e. Indian. Before Rakhi 'discovers' the journals, she has been creating a sense of 'homeland' through photos of India and other images available through globalized networks of communication. She is a painter and she creates for herself an 'imagined

India' through these images.Haunted by that horrible events and the experience of quest for her root, Rakhi finds unexpected gifts such as the possibility of new love through her father and understanding for her family. Divakaruni effectively takes the readers into the light of parental bond and the quest for the protagonist's roots.

The Mirror of Fire and Dreaming (2005) is the second novel of the Brotherhood-trilogy. Here, the master storyteller takes us from the original beauty of Himalaya to the world of an ancient kingdom, full of colourful Indian valleys and aromas. The novel *The Palace of Illusions* (2006) takes the reader to the time of great Indian epic The Mahabharata which is historical, mythical and magical. However, the novel has its relation to today's war-torn world. Through the female narrator Panchali, Divakaruni gives a rare feminine interpretation of the epic. *The Mahabharata* is retold from the point of view of an amazing woman Panchali, the wife of the Pandavas who were cheated by their step brothers Kauravas.

The eleventh novel written by Divakaruni is *One Amazing Thing* (2010). It is another fine example of Divakaruni's art of storytelling. It received great praise. In it, a group of nine people from entirely different backgrounds, religion, race, nationality, appearance and status are shown trapped in the building of visa office at an Indian consulate after a massive earthquake in an American city.

Oleander Girl (2013) is the latest novel by Divakaruni. It is an exploration of identity through relationship. In this novel, Korobi Roy, the protogonist is raised by her loving grandparents in India, and given with a good life. She gets engaged to the handsome Rajat, the only son of a high-profile family, ready to embark on a new life. But, on the night of their engagement, Korobi's grandfather passes away making her discover a shocking secret, one that will change everything she thought she know about herself, and the people who loved her. Shattered by this discovery and by her grandparents' betrayal, Korobi undertakes a courageous search across post- 9/11 America to find her true identity. Her dramatic, startling journey ultimately thrusts her into the most difficult situation in her life.

Apart from poems and fiction, she has also mastered the art of non-fiction too. She writes a column for the magazine *India Today* entitled *Stars and Spice* which deals with the issues of the women characters. She has edited an anthology *Multitude: Cross Cultural Readings for Writers* (1993) which includes stories about cross-cultural communication, expectations of friendship, the 1992 Los-Angeles riots, and prejudice against gay gender. She has written a regular column Spice of Life for the online magazine *Salon* (from mid-1997 to early 1998). Also, she has written aplay in 1998 entitled *Clothes* which was performed by the Neo-World Theatre at Amherst College and at the International Drama Festival Athens, Greece in 1999.Thus, Chitra Banerjee Divakaruni has proved herself as an eminent writer and novelist.

Amongst the other leading writers of Indian heritage, writing in English. Mostly she writes about the turbulence of the women which is impacted by relationships. Women portrayed by her are exploited, subjugated and marginalized by the dominance of male community. These are the women who experience the brunt of sufferings when they cross the magical circle drawn around them by their home-culture. Her women struggle to create their own identity out of their relational existence. The hardship that these women face while fighting against the established order of the society, shattering experiences of womanhood, inflicted subordination, class conflicts, social censorship, gender discrimination, female infanticide and financial issues like dowry system are explored from a woman's perspective.

Divakaruni's journey from the state of a young Indian graduate to that of a writer in America seems to be a complete circle. She left India at the age of nineteen, which means she must have known India enough though she became an immigrant later in America. Therefore, she is able to write about India, so much like an outsider. Most of her works are either set in Calcutta, her biological home, or in California, America, her current land. Her writings are a mixture of her own knowledge about India and her experiences as an immigrant. She is well-versed in both the cultures that she has expressed them in her literary works. Divakaruni often puts her female protagonists into the two entirely different cultures. She brings forward the contrast between the restricted existence of women in India and the possible freedom and liberation in America through human relationships, a land of free- culture. The concept of freedom and independence is always the prime focus of her writing. Her female protagonists are deeply rooted in relationship with family and the surrounding. When they are subjugated they strive hard to break off the shackles around them and prove their individuality as liberated women.

Divakaruni highlights how a woman views herself when she faces problems, and other women and their problems as well. She wants her women to view themselves as human beings and not simply as women only. She is of the view that women are not mere puppets or the sex objects for momentary pleasure, but they are equal to men with feelings and emotions. Almost every work of art by her ventures deep into women's psyche and explores the nature and scope of the trauma of women's life.

She demands women emancipation and tries to create a humanistic attitude towards women when they are interwined in relationships. She also makes it sure that the traditional concepts of stereotypes are changed, and the definition of virtue of modern women. Human relationships are the form of behavioral practices and exchanges between or with people in different spheres and affairs of life. Many attempts have been made and various dimensions of thoughts have been exercised to understand human relationships from literal, philosophical, social and psychological positions focusing on human instincts and its multiple expressions connecting with surroundings.

Yet, it appears that human relationship is a complex and complicated phenomenon. It is a complicated task to define and understand human relationship because it is always in constant change according to the emerging situation and changes in society.

The continuous societal changes taking place in the society extremely influence human relationships from various perspectives. The external factors and forces which are emanating due to various changes at local and global level are credited to bringing changes at personal and social levels in human relationships. These changes formulate social and ideological norms by which humans are subjected to accept or reject changes according to their convenience. The socially, ideologically driven and explicably loaded bond that people share with one another is always in transformative mode and function as a tool to bring changes in the societal values. In order to have a clear understanding of human relationships, it is essential to consider some of the definitions related to it. The mediocre understanding of human relationships is understood as one's relationship or association with another person. It seems to suggest how an individual man or woman is related or connected to another man or woman.

In general, it can be stated how people interact and move with each other when they come together in a group or family or in a larger systematic organization. In academic context, human relationships examine human behavior at a workplace and then use systematic knowledge to analyze and suggest necessary efforts needed to maintain and enhance the performance of humans. From religious and spiritual point of view, human relationship means to recognize, respect and also safeguard the dignity of every individual along with his or her sincere efforts and significant contribution made for the achievement of human goals. The layman's observation on human relationships leads us to have a common understanding of its ingredients which assist us to know it in a better way.

From nineteenth to twenty first century the concept of human relationships has undergone various changes because of many psycho-social and technological changes. These changes have shifted the attention from God to man, universal to individual, international to national and from global to local. It is worthwhile to consider some definition stated by scholars and critics in relation to human relationships. According to Robert Owen in his book The Quest for New Moral World: 'Human relationship is an interaction and co-operation of people in a group' (52). Owen's opinion on human relationships originates from contemporary idea involving humans in the world. His usage of the word 'group' seems to comprise different institutions like family, home, business, company, government, association, university, hospital, church and trust.

The American Book Award winner Chitra Divakaruni's new novel, *Oleander Girl*, features a young woman from a distinguished and orthodox Bengali heritage. She falls in love with a man from a nouveau-riche business family in Kolkata, a city buffeted by the clash between the old and new ways of life. On the brink of marriage, she discovers a family secret which shakes up her sense of self, causes her to put off her wedding, and impels her on a journey to America which in turn ultimately transforms her in a drastic manner she never imagined. Set in 2002, in the fraught world of post 9/11 America and India torn apart by the Godhra Riots, *Oleander Girl* is an examination of the consequences of intolerance and the cost of desire.

Chitra Banerjee Divakaruni brings social awareness to the readers through her writing. Apart from pointing out social issues such as racism, gender bias and generation gap, she has in this novel brilliantly dealt with the theme of parental relationship with children, in spite of the fact that her novels represent the contemporary diasporic literature. She is a modern novelist and her backgrounds are the contemporary India and the United States. Her novels connect with the present existence of life emphasizing human relationships irrespective of lands. Her writing is critically acclaimed for being popular among readers.

The novel *Oleander Girl* depicts the challenging journey taken up by the protagonist in order to find her roots. The objective of this chapter is to explore the quest for roots and parental ties in the novels *Oleander Girl* and *Queen of Dreams*. Korobi, an orphan is the protagonist in the novel *Oleander* Girl around whom the narrative revolves. She is raised by her grandparents. Bimal Roy, a conservative old man and a retired barrister is her grandfather. Sarojini, a warm-hearted person and the grandmother of Korobi. She yearns for her parents‘ love during her childhood days. When Anu, Karobi's mother had been pregnant with Karobi, she entangles in an argument with her father and dies of a tragic fall after giving birth to Karobi. Her father also died in a car crash three months before her mother's death are what conveyed to Karobi about her parents. Women in India are conservative to some extent, they experience psychological challenges, face emotional imbalance and the challenges of non-acceptance of mystery.

To achieve self-contentment, they grapple for their identities. Divakurini's novel *Oleander Girl* too portrays Korobi's untiring efforts towards self-rediscovery amidst these odds. This novel is a narration of Korobi's endeavour to find out her roots. Divakaruni speaks for the young Korobi who leaves her native land India and travels for America, an entirely new land. A multi- faceted story of rediscovery, Oleander Girl is a part mystery, part search, but mostly the story of a young girl striving to find her parental roots and to know where she belongs.

'Korobi' means 'oleander' in Bengali. She wonders why her mother named her after a plant which is beautiful but poisonous. Divakaruni exhibits Korobi as an ordinary girl, impulsive and thoughtful. She loves Rajat, a successful and wealthy man who is engaged to her. When her loving grandfather dies unexpectedly after hiding all the secrets about her parents, her grandmother's impulsion urges her to reveal the truth making Karobi to have the quest for the truth about her parental roots. She leaves all her comforts to find out the truth about her father and herself.

The protagonist Korobi goes through a change in her personality both mentally and physically and faces many challenges in her journey. The *Oleander Girl*'s story takes the readers through the thought process, a negotiation between desires and consequences. This novel attempts to describe Divakaruni's concern for modern youth. The novel inspires youth to stand up for their own identity in life. The theme of the novel advocates the fact that one should know one's roots and family heritage. The character of Korobi's conveys the author's message for the youth of today to possess courage to discover and accept the realities of theie identity.

Korobi is a dynamic and charismatic young Indian woman who comes to terms with her life and finds herself in America to explore the roots of her lineage. She is an attractive girl brought up by her grandparents in a typical Hindu traditional way. She is from a renowned family in Calcutta. The road in which their house is located is named after her great- grandfather Tarak Prasad Roy. Her conservative and traditional grandfather provides Korobi an extremely protected environment. Korobi loves her grandparents and also respects them in every possible way. She has imbibed traditional values and does not have any exposure to the lives of other youngsters in the city. Her family background, her intelligence and upbringing give Korobi the perfect aura of a traditional girl. She has a friend called Mimi through whom she meets Rajat at a party. Rajat develops a fascination for Korobi as she appears traditional and belongs to a good family.

Korobi lives a cocooned life under the protection of her grandfather at every step. She is sent to a boarding school for education and is hidden from the outer world and its fascination. She has longed for her parents when as a child.

Her grandparents are too conservative at times but she knows that their love has always provided the best for her. Her distress when her grandfather dies is aptly captured by Divakaruni in the following line:"Grandfather exited my life like a bullet, leaving a bleeding hole behind" (OG 48).

Though Karobi is bound to tradition she is a rebel too. When her grandfather decides her marriage without her approval, she cringes and takes it out on him. Her grandfather becomes furious when Karobi decides to wear a trendy dress instead of a traditional attire even for grand occasions. He compares the dress that she wears to that of an ill-reputed woman. Yet, she stands up for her decisions and choices and never regrets them.

When Korobi visualizes her mother in her dream one morning, she fears to disclose it to her grandfather. She says: "From time to time, I imagined- a mix of horror and pride- what Grandfather's reaction would be when he saw me in it" (OG 18). After her engagement and her grandfather's death, Karobi learns the truth about her parents. The truth and the loss completely ruin her peace. Through her grandmother she learns that her mother Anu went to America for higher studies and fell in love with a foreigner named Rob Lancey during her stay there.

Anu had been pregnant because of her premarital relationship with Rob. She longed to be with her parents in India during pregnancy and took permission from her father and flew to her hometown to spend the happiest times of her pregnancy with her parents. She hoped to make the visit a memorable one by convincing her father to allow her to marry Rob during her stay in India but he denied her permission even to return to America. As the conversation resulted in an argument, she unexpectedly slipped from the staircase and started bleeding and this ended in a tragedy. She was taken to the hospital where Korobi was born. Unfortunately her mother passed away. When Korobi discovers the whole truth, she feels shattered and moves out of her sheltered lifestyle in Kolkatta. She tells Rajat:

"I'm so confused. All the things I was so proud of, my family, my

heritage- they're only half- true. The other half of me- I don't know

anything about it. Except that all this time my father was alive, and in

America" (*OG* 66).

Rajat is very caring and loving towards Karobi. He basically loves his parents and adores his sister. He is popular among friends and quite jovial too. The servants admire him for his generosity. Rajat in his heart respects the Indian traditions. He likes and regards Karobi's grandparents Sarojini and Bimal. He is fond of talking about the family history and the story of the old house of Karobi's grandfather. Sarojini and Bimal recognise this and admire him for his qualities. Rajat is sensible, worldly and pretends to be liberal. When Korobi comes to him with the truth about her lineage, he accepts her but does not want her to pursue the matter further. He is not idealistic and does not proactively seek the truth. But when Korobi is adamant in finding the truth about her parental roots, he helps her.

Korobi leavesfor America to find her father and his past after knowing the fact that her real roots lie in the United States across the ocean. It is very difficult to find her father as she knows only his first name and has no photograph of him either. Still she expresses her strong desire to know about her own father to Rajat. In a foreign land, she determines to take up the challenge of exploring the whereabouts of her father. She never wants to get tangled in this relationship and puts aside her marriage plans. Although she is insisted upon to marry first, she determines to find her roots and prioritizes that.

By explaining about the minimum possibilities in finding her father, Rajat tries to persuade her but she still says: “I don’t care!” (OG 71). Korobi is determined to fly to America and she asserts: “I’m even prepared to go to America” (OG 72). Korobi decides to give up her peaceful, satisfying and secured life in Kolkata and gets ready to sacrifice even her love in order to find her roots by choosing a challenging path and ventures to America after assuming the difficulties she is likely to face.

Without knowing her real roots, Korobi goes through hard times during her stay in America. She is a wilful, charismatic young woman and is unafraid of people and their comments. Divakaruni describes her as a fearless woman. She just wants to follow her heart and boldly declares, "But neither do I want to be a trouble to you. I understand how much of a problem for you my heritage has become... If it is so important for your business, I’m willing to release Rajat from the engagement" (OG 79).

Korobi encounters many problems during her search and faces the real cruel world in the US. However, her inner strength and confidence emerge when she faces difficult situations. Protected by her grandparents throughout her life, she only now finds the real thorny world but still, she composes herself and moves forward. Korobi hires Desai, a private detective to help her search . She learns that her mother was in the University of Berkeley and her father’s first name is Rob and they had studied together.

In the United States, Korobi using the old photograph of her mother along with a friend of hers advertises in an Indian newspaper that anyone who comes up with any information about Anu Roy would be rewarded. Korobi pursues her search with a great deal of determination. Desai, the detective gives her three leads –one in Boston and two other people in California named Rob who had been in the University of Berkeley at the same time as her mother. During the course of the search, she runs out of money in New York. However, paucity of funds does not deter Korobi. She goes to the US with very little money and stays with Mitra, Rajat's manager, a very unfriendly person.still, She is not afraid;she optimistically takes on the situation as it comes. She is committed to finding the truth about her father and she has come this far away from her own people. When she does not have enough money, she decides to sell her hair for her search which makes her feel even more confident and thus she declares: "I feel light-headed, untethered. But once the money is in my hand I'm somewhat consoled. I now have enough for California; I have done it without having to beg anyone" (OG 177). Thus the immense courage of young Karobi is commendably portrayed by Divakaruni.

Earlier when Korobi planed to travel to California in search of her father, she realized that she was penniless. Desai suggests to seek help from her fiancé. But she denies to ask any money from anyone especially Rajat because she wants to make it on her own, and she is quite stubborn about it. She says: "I'll get the money, I say with jaunty rashness, though I have no idea how. I know this much, though: I'm not going to ask Rajat" (OG 172). The protagonist is self- dependent and has self- respect. Though she has the opportunity of asking for favour she takes the responsibility of it on her shoulders.

Chitra Banerjee's concern and sympathy lies for the women. Mitra who is arranged by Rajat to pick Korobi up from the airport does not turn up and this is the first disappointment faced by Korobi. She faces numerous other hardships starting with this. Korobi is assisted by Desai, a detective agent. He is appointed by Rajat to help in finding her father. She also gets acquainted with Vic, Desai's nephew who is a part- time assistant. The only one who understands Korobi's feelings is Vic. To find Korobi's father, he offers his support. Three names are shortlisted by him: Rob Mariner, an estate lawyer in San Francisco, Rob Evanston, an architect, and Rob Davis, a writer in the Santacruz Club. To her disappointment, when she meets them in person, she finds that they are in no way related to her. One thinks that she is out there for money while another tries to sexually harass her. She is almost ready to give up as these experiences shatter her willpower. After meeting Meera Anand, Korobi's hope revives as Meera acknowledges that she knows her mother Anu Roy. With the hope that she can reach her father, she manages all the difficult situations as an immigrant. In her every action she gets directed towards her quest:

This seems like a small sacrifice, but for a traditional girl whose

marriage is fixed, this is a big step. But for Korobi, it comes naturally;

she boldly goes ahead and gives up her hair for her dream. (*OG* 94-95)

Korobi takes every chance to get some clue about her father. She meets Rob Mariner alone at his home though she knows that it is quite risky. True to her apprehensions, Mariner takes advantage when seeing Korobi alone but she does not panic. She faces the situation bravely, and her valour saves her. Even after such an experience she does not give up and continues to search for her father. Korobi's biggest strengths are her values and ethics. She has the ability to stand by her convictions amidst adversity which is admirable.

Although there is a wonderful opportunity for Korobi to get married to Rajat and settle in life, her pursuit of truth jeopardizes everything. She decides to go against a tide of adversity. Her thoughts are: "It would be cowardly, for the sake of security, to relinquish this chance to find and to know the man my mother loved so much" (OG 78). But she does not want to go to a family which respects her only for her lineage since it is based on falsehood. She thinks that she cannot "pull the blanket of status quo over myself, and dwindle into a wife" (OG 217).

Korobi tells Rajat that she is ready to face the repercussions but never wants to give in for the safety of the fallacy. She finds that her father is an African-American and also that her parents were never married. She tells all the truth about her to the Bose family as she does not want to live a falsified life. She is a perfect example of a determined woman who is educated and confident and also has conviction about her ideas. She stands up courageously for truth. She convinces Rajat to let her rediscover her roots by herself. Earlier he does not accept this but later he bows down as he sees her determination. He falls in love with the simple and intriguing Korobi and loves her traditional way of life with her guarding grandparents.

Karobi shares this with her grandmother and says that when she looks herself in the mirror, she sees her skin, hair and everything differently. There is a new identity of her being a half-Black as she is the daughter of Rob Lancey, an African-American father. When she meets her actual father, Korobi gets to know about his life with her mother, Anu. She learns another bitter unacceptable truth that her mother and father were never married and Karobi was not born out of wedlock. Korobi is unable to digest this fact and feels extremely shameful about her. Her father tells Korobi that Anu had promised Bimal Roy that she would never marry against her father's wishes.

To keep the promise which she made to her father, she had not agreed to marriage even after repeated requisition. Korobi is disillusioned about her otherness and her alteration. She thinks: "Some kinds of success are worse than failure. It would have been better not to have found my father than to live with this profound shame" (*OG* 246). Divakaruni describes Korobi as a woman who is dealing with her life with new identity after her return to India. The Bose family does not accept her new identity as an illegitimate daughter. She decides to pursue her studies and amazes her grandmother with her transformation. Her trans-cultural experience makes her a new empowered woman.

In America, Korobi gets easily adjusted to its way of life but at the same time she does not forget her root and promises. She says: "I was the granddaughter of Bimal Roy... because like my mother I had made certain promises" (*OG* 170). She gets attracted to Vic who understands and supports her in all her endeavours and is tempted to continue her life with him when he approaches her during her stay in America. She loves the place and has a choice to stay back. She says: "I'll have to make my new decision: Vic or Rajat, America or India" (OG 218).

However, she goes back to India with the same values that she imbibed from her traditional upbringing. Knowing what is right for her and resisting temptations, she returns as a better person. She becomes the beautiful oleander that her mother wanted her to be, she unties herself from the web of identity crisis. A sense of fulfilment is achieved by Karobi. A different dimension to existence is opened up by her newly -found facts. Even when facing a set back while she is abandoned by Rajat, Korobi's courage and stubbornness enable her to keep going without any disappointments. She is rejected by Rajat and his mother as they could not accept the changes in Korobi's attire, haircut and her attitude after she returns to India. But, Korobi is bold enough to face the trial and returns Rajat's engagement ring with dignity.

Korobi receives frequent calls from her father and Vic who invite her to America but her mind wants to stay in her own country. She says: "I can't deny that America's siren song had pulled at me. But I came back, of my own choice. Surely that counts for some-thing. I love my mother. But I am not her. My journey has taught me that" (*OG* 280).

Korobi is a strong woman who does not heed to the temptations. She is crystal clear about her mission in America as she discovers her root. She proves to be different from her mother Anu by resisting her temptations. During that period of time the families get reconciled and patch up.

Rajat and Korobi's wedding ceremony is well organised. Rajat's family realises her true and genuine love for Rajat and the fact that she tries not to hide anything about her true identity eventually brings her close to Rajat's family. The visit she pays to their art gallery in New York to help the Bose family makes the family realize the courage and conviction. Korobi accepts her roots and her alterity as the daughter of mixed blood, mixed race and not as a child born out of wed-lock. Her good nature and passionate love for Rajat make Bose's family accept her identity as the granddaughter of Bimal Roy and also an African-American father's daughter. Divakaruni voices out for a woman and her race in the most intricate way possible and her narrative style clasps the reader's heart and soul. One such Divakaruni's novel *Oleander Girl* which ends on a happy note. The readers realize that Korobi is true to her name, an Oleander Girl who is beautiful and also tough. Her journey to find her father and her determination to go against all the odds make her reach out to what she wants. Her way of handling the crises of her life, her resistance to America's temptation and Vic and strong urge to follow her heart, irrespective of the reaction of people around her make the readers appreciate the novel from a feminist perspective.

Korobi's trans-cultural journey exposes the ways of her life in the Eastern and the Western world, making her more confident. The cultural clashes experienced by her is also one of the reasons for her strong attitude as a woman. The traditional Bengali culture creates the foundation of her living and the liberal American culture teaches her to understand the intentions of her grandfather who wanted to protect the women of his family with his expectations and promised to bind them. She is now in a better position to appreciate the goodness that life has offered her in a better way.

The story connects women of three generations- Korobi the youngest, Korobi's mother Anu, and Korobi's grandmother Sarojini, in which each generation has a unique womanhood experiences. One can witness the constant clash between Korobi's traditional upbringings and to be a part of Rajat's modern family. Her struggle in balancing these two brings out the tensions in her family and also Rajat's, forcing her to choose between security and the rediscovery of her 'self'. Divakaruni focuses on the conflict between Indian identity and transnational location which is a conflict between individual desire and social norms through human relationships. Her novel is a thrust of female identity and women freedom which is a question lying behind. Basic convictions and values drive a person's behaviour as he or she faces difficult situations. They drive, motivate and keep a person in the right path. Korobi's education and core values dictate her actions when she stands at the cross- roads of life. She knows that her future is at stake but still she is not prepared to trade her conscience for her happiness. Divakaruni presents Korobi as a modest woman who at all costs journeys to find her origin. Through Karobi's character one can acknowledge that today's youth has a bold and rational approach towards their life similar to Karobi.

Divakurni's characters have the courage to leave their perfect life towards an adventurous quest for truth. Her protagonists trigger the readers to think. She attributes strong will-power to Karobi who acquires enough valour to fulfil her venture successfully. Her *Oleander Girl* leaves the readers a message that is to know the truth about oneself which is very significant in life, and to get at this truth, one has to have the courage to face the troubles in life. One should not throw up one's hands in air in despair about the truth they need to learn; rather they should muster courage to turn things to their way.

Most of her novels give an opportunity to understand the protagonist's quest for identifying the roots and identity in the world. This marks Chitra Banerjee Divakurini as a prominent writer and a one considerate about women.

The life of the women characters standing in between the two worlds and the ambivalence towards dual belongingness between the homeland and the host are brought to limelight very interestingly. To nurture her parental relationship and her own life she risks her very existence and succeeds in a new environment. Most of the women characters of Divakaruni are tested in the conflict in human relationship. Hence,the quest for roots through human relationships is one of the major themes of her novel.

In contrast to the other women characters, the protagonist of this novel traverses from one place to another in search of her roots. In India, she has to protect the family bondage, culture and tradition and keep up strict discipline and her overprotected life does not let her to decide anything on her own. But when circumstances force her to find her real-self she finds her real roots by herself amidst many hurdles; the foreign land draws her towards individuality and moulds her to become stronger enough to discover her 'self'.

Divakaruni offers empowerment for women at various levels including solidarity with other women and acknowledgment of the supportive role women often play both individually and communally. She challenges the traditional gender bias which is an expectation of South-Asian men in many occasions. This indicates the questions of multiple assumptions based on gender which are not the only thing affecting women. The strong female characters in Divakaruni's novels acquire independence, autonomy and success which served as a support system through human relationships.

South Asian women are portrayed as successful women-as Indians, as Americans, as individuals, and as members of their new communities. She also emphasizes on accepting the true origin of roots and acknowledge what it has to offer. Korobi rediscovers her 'self' concerning the grappling journey that she attempts courageously despite all the hurdles that come on her way. A society gets mirrored through a family that provides strong building blocks for an individual contributing to renovate a strong society and nation.

Family is important in everyone's life because it is the basic unit of society. Without family there cannot be any stronger bond in an individual's life. People with family support and happy relationships give confidence and success in their lives. The flaws are those which break the ties within the family itself. Misunderstandings, miscommunication and envious feelings lead to familial conflicts. Chitra Banerjee Divakaruni weaves an amazing tale of intricate, intertwined, and intimate relationships by highlighting the themes of reconciliation in search for parental root in the novel *Queen of Dreams.*

The author symbolises death as a retirement from the world through Mrs. Gupta, the mother of the protagonist Rakhi. The trauma of the protagonist Rakhi is that only after her mother's death does she strive to discover the truth by knitting the bonds herself that she had discarded. The second half of the chapter focuses on the theme of reconciliation that explores the relationship of various characters that distance and alienate the relations, isolation and strenuous relations followed by a critical study of the protagonist's parental roots.

Marriage and family are the important institutions of a society that provide emotional, physical and social support to individuals. Family is the first school for a child and the mother is the first teacher. Developing a healthy relationship by inculcating, imbibing and nurturing values in their children is the main duty of parents. The husband and wife have equal responsibility to love and care for each other and their children. As mentioned in The Bible, "Children are a heritage of the Lord" (Psalms 127:3). The sacred duty of parents is to rear their children in love and righteousness by providing their physical and spiritual needs, teaching them with love to serve one another, to observe the rules of society and to be law-abiding citizens where they live. The parents should take the responsibility and invest their heart and soul into rearing their children.

Nobody wishes to be a part of tumultuous and vulnerable family where there is misunderstanding, stress, high expectations, mistrust, alienated feeling, isolation, financial, social or physical problems, lack of freedom or personal space and so on. Separation and break ups in a family may occur at times. However, the universal fact is that human beings crave to be with their family and share their moments of success, happiness, grief or even death. sustaining a good family life is not easy; people have to use both their head and heart to make sure that their relationships are strong.

Indians in the recent time face problems like relocation, reconciliation and assimilation. Reconciliation involves building a better relationship among people who cannot connect because of their misunderstandings and differences. One thing that human beings have to accept in life is change. People are unprepared for this stage in life. True reconciliation has its own unique features that are not about a simple excuse. It involves restoration, acceptance of one's weakness and growth.

The one to be forgiven first is the strongest and the person who forgives is the happiest. This reconciliation concept is strongly highlighted by Divakaruni in her best accomplished novel *Queen of Dreams*. She crafts an amazing tale of parental relationships depicting its highs and lows. A family life gets complicated when it comes with a lot of baggage. From the origin of human civilization upto globalization, people from all walks of life crave for familial love, attention and affection.

Divakaruni paints the need for love and support in the family through the reconciliation of broken ties in a very natural and spontaneous way through the protagonist's life. Rakhi struggles individually with an aim of rediscovering the purpose of her life. Divakaruni has written *Queen of Dreams* where she paints a caring image of Rakhi's mother Mrs. Gupta who is a dream interpreter. She visualizes a snake in her dream and feels worried about it. The snake in her dream alarms her as she believes that it is there to foretell a great change. She fears that something bad is going to happen in her household. Her anxiety and prayer are evident through her words: "Don't let it be Rakhi, Sonny or Jonaki. Don't let it be my husband whom I have failed in many ways" (*QD* 2).

She is a protective mother who does not want to risk the lives of her immediate family members and thus prefers to sacrifice her own life as the situation demands it. She takes the responsibility as a wife and mother towards her family members. She serves her husband as a wife. Rakhi too as a child has blossomed with the love and care showered by her mother and father. She says: At dinner Father admired the creative shapes we'd made and said it was a meal at once delicious and instructive. He cleaned up the kitchen afterward, humming a Hindi song as he scrubbed the sink with Comet, his hands encased in Neon Yellow Rubber one, always kind with music. (*QD* 231)

Divakaruni emphasizes the issue of Rakhi's mother and father's relationship in the family environment which impacts Rakhi's completely developed personality. This starts when she sees her mother sleeping alone always in a room. She says: "My mother always sleeps alone" (*QD* 239).

They stay together in the same house as a family but there is a big gap in their hearts. Every day after telling a tale or listening to Rakhi's tales, her mother used to kiss her and go to Rakhi's father's room, just talk to him, close the door and go to the sewing room to sleep alone. At the young age of just eight, Rakhi never understands anything about her family's lifestyle but curiosity leads her to observe the functioning of a typical family life. She explores deep in her friends' houses about the ways and arrangements about a real family life which is different from hers.

One afternoon when she goes to play in her classmate's house, she gets to know something strange. Her friend tells her not to jump on her parents' bed. Rakhi gets shocked know this. She asks her friend: "You mean your mother sleeps here – with your dad?' I asked surprised and faintly disgusted" (*QD* 134). When the girl replies "yes", she feels quite strange. After this incident she goes to her friend's home casually to monitor the sleeping arrangements of her parents and finally concludes that her family is weird. This deeply affects her innocent mind.

She asks her mother: "Why don't you sleep with dad? I kept asking, or at least with me, like Mallika's mother does? Don't you love us?"(199) and her mother replies that though she loves them, she cannot sleep with them because she is a dream-teller and she cannot concentrate on it if someone is in bed with her. Rakhi gets confused and shocked but her curiosity is not pacified. The words of Mrs. Gupta reveals that she is giving her profession of dream- telling more priority in comparison to her daughter, husband and family life.

Divakaruni reveals the same factors by showing the observations which her protagonist Rajhi has made of her mother from childhood. "Rakhi is suspicious, secretive and silent. She turns to be a pessimist, who finds fault with almost everyone she knows" (*QD* 211). Rakhi says: "My mother- secretive, stubborn, and unreliable – couldn't hold a tune to save her life. I wanted to be just like her" (QD 213). This results in her divorce or separation from Sonny, her husband. Rakhi admits that a relationship cannot be spoilt in one night like milk. There will be hints for a while, but she chooses not to see them. Relationships in a family turn sour when turmoil arises. The family environment leaves a deep impact in shaping her personality as well as her life. She becomes introvert, sensitive and secretive similar to her mother. In Rakhi's eye, everything and everyone is directly linked against her, including her husband, Sonny a popular DJ in town.

When it comes to her marital life, she follows her mother's advice that one should not be dependent on the other and that is not termed as pure love. She tries to live her life without Sonny's help in anything and is deeply impressed by her mother. She is separated and live as a single parent having a seven year old daughter named Jonaki, an artist struggling by profession and an entrepreneur of a failing coffee shop in Berkeley, California, trying to maintain her career and family life in an independent manner. But her family life is imbalanced when she could not relate to her family members at the emotional level. Rakhi wants to be like her mother. She wishes to read dreams in the same manner as her mother. But she is not successful here also as she is not gifted with the power of dream- telling and does not know much about her mother which remains a long-term secret.

She accepts her parents' discordant relationship and tries to probe into her father's life without going close to him. She does not realize his pain and loneliness until her father translates the dreams of her mother in her journals that she writes. Rakhi reveals: Her mother's dream journals offer her with few revelations: She was an orphan chosen by an aunt who also had the power of dream-telling. She had seen the same in Mrs. Gupta, and took her along to the dream caves where she could refine her gift to help the society. Rakhi understands her mother's pain of breaking away from her family which would not have been easy for her because she loved her family so much. She sacrificed the joys of her personal life by upholding her professional one. After knowing about all this, Rakhi feels relieved and starts to understand her father. Divakaruni emphasizes on the importance of family relationships and support to lead one's life in a seamless manner.

Reconciliation in family relationships is cleverly knitted through Mrs. Gupta's sudden death and the horror of 9/11 tragedy. Family is not only a source of true happiness but also a refuge where one gains strength and support at the time of hardship. When Rakhi's mother passes away, her ex-husband Sonny makes sure to handle Rakhi's family life well. He takes responsibility by treating Rakhi's home like his own. He supports in Rakhi's career by suggesting tips to improve it. He brings back their daughter Jonaki home so that Rakhi gets a chance to nurture and groom herself to be a responsible individual in the society and would help her to take her mind off from her mother's immediate and unexpected death.

Her father Mr. Gupta's personality is never liked by her and consciously she maintains distance and tries to stand without her family's help when the Chai house comes on a sale. But, she is rendered her father's encouragement financially, emotionally and physically when her business gradually crashes. He helps Rakhi to re-establish the Chai house with a new name, "Kurma House". She reopens it and waits for the customers where Sonny enters first and places the order for her surprise and further brings his band and DJ team as customers. Sonny supports her in this way indirectly. Thus the reconciliation process takes place among Mr. Gupta, Sonny and Rakhi. All forget and forgive and stay united at the time of crisis. Rakhi feels happy from within.

One night she finds herself thanking Sonny for saving her life. He takes her hand and says that he is happy for what little he is able to do at that point of time. He asks her to come to the club again and hear him like her first going to see him. She says neither yes nor no. She bends forward a little to allow him to kiss her cheek before he leaves. She goes to his club standing in the long line, waits for the doors to open and musters all her courage to tell Sonny that she has come to hear him. She likes everything there and enjoys a lot unlike before. She dances her way and feels contented to enjoy this transient mote of glitter- dust on the web of the world where Sonny touches orbits once more. The restoration of the central characters – Rakhi and Sonny is a miracle which was for sometime lost in between them.

Forgiveness and repentance again act as a pillar between Rakhi and her father. Since they are a family, the chance of hurting each other increases more with the passage of time. Divakaruni's characters develop a strong reconciling habit that breaks all barriers and offers hope to survive in a new world. The family remains as a binding force in all these circumstances that connects the past and present, the old and the new. It is easy to separate the bond with a little energy but it is hard for one to separate a familial bond that is invisible and simultaneously intertwined. This fact is brought out by Divakaruni through her wisely crafted tale *Queen of Dreams.* Divakaruni refines the theme of reconciliation through the protagonist Rakhi. In an interview Divakaruni expresses:

'Women in particular respond to my work because I am writing about

them, women in love, in difficulties, women in relationships. I want

people to relate to my characters, to feel their joy and pain, because it

will be harder to be prejudice when they meet them in real life'.

Rakhi's life stresses on the significance of family in an individual's life. Rakhi as a struggling individual does not want to accept or seek for the support of her family in matters related to her but tragedies bring them together; she sheds her ego and drops her pride by reconciling with her family whole heartedly as she understands the fact that when life crashes down, family alone would support and help to regain happiness. She experiences the bliss of completeness when she reunites with her family. It shows that family relationships always come first, and remain forever.

Divakaruni proves that reconciliation leads to familial bonding in *Queen of Dreams*. Though the protagonist Rakhi is born and brought up in the US, her inner self is unpolluted by Americanness or any such trait that is un–Indian. Her mother Mrs.Gupta, the dream- teller converts her foreign living space to a space of dreams rooted in Indian cultural belief. Though Mrs. Gupta never tells anything to Rakhi, the life experiences of her dreams echo and re-echo the soul of India. Dream invades the major portion of the space of the novel and the material space is subordinated to the enlarged space of the dream. Dreams, dream journals, and dream-telling in the novel *Queen of Dreams* germinate from the oriental cultural belief system.

In the novel, dream signifies the female defence psychology, a safe space or refuge or retreat from which the female resists or seeks liberation from the anxiety, fear and feeling of insecurity associated with the fragile sensibility of sex which is characteristic of the Indian female mind. In the diasporic situation of internationalization, the fragile female sensibility of sex is shaken and it ends in a divorce as in the case of Rakhi or seeks asylum in the vocation of dream- telling that prescribes negation of sex as a necessity. The dreams, dream journals and dream-telling implicitly and explicitly demonstrate the anxiety of the female over her sexual integrity, which she fears would be spoiled and despoiled by mixing with females and males of different national and racial identities. In the first episode from the dream journals and in the subsequent episodes, 'cave' is a recurring motif. The snake that makes its presence felt in the first episode causes anxiety and fear, which signifies the feeling of insecurity that lies beneath the 'female breast:

The dream stimulates anxiety and a feeling of insecurity. The snake in the symbol-lexicon signifies the male genital organ whereas the cave that is a recurrent motif in all dream episodes signifies the female genital cavity. But snake in this particular dream –episode foretells death. For Mrs. Gupta, retired from the sexual life unilaterally for the sacred cause of dream- telling, male sexuality is a dreadful experience interlocked with a sense of guilt and death. The excuse for failing her husband, denying him marital sex for the sacred cause of dream-telling does not redeem her of her guilt. So the snake that evokes the sensibility incites the death anxiety also.

In The Bible, the wages of sexual sin is death, but in approved marital life, the wages for abstinence from sex is death. Dream is an inner psychic activity and the vague apprehensions of danger subsist in the interior space of dream. The feeling of insecurity is a complex emerging from anxiety, interacting with the external material situations of hostility. Rakhi also has the experience of dreams: "I dreamed a great deal during those years and often my dreams were suffocatingly intense. I'd wake from them with my heart pounding so hard I thought it might burst"

(QD 5).

During her early years Rakhi asks her mother, "Why don't you sleep with dad, or at least with me like Mallika's mother does? Don't you love us?" (QD 7). Her mother replies:

"I do love you; I don't sleep with your father because my work is to

dream. I can't do it if someone is in bed with me... I dream the dreams

of other people so I can help them live their live" (*QD* 7).

Even when she keeps herself away from her husband and daughter she claims that she loves her daughter "I do love you" is an assertive statement, on her love for her daughter but the fact that the conjugal love is wilfully frustrated is not denied.

Since the mother in Divakaruni's *The Queen of Dreams* possesses the mysterious ability of mind reading and dream-telling, her cognitive capabilities can be considered unusual, even superhuman. Rakhi perceives her own ordinary human cognition as inferior and uninteresting. Yet the daughter's ability to make assumptions about her mother's facial expressions, tones of voice and other paralinguistic signals is anything but trivial. It is an inherent communication skill, which cognitive psychologists and philosophers refer to as' Theory of Mind' or mind reading.

It suggests that humans possess the inherent ability to make assumptions and predictions regarding the mental states of others on the basis of observable body language, tone of voice, and other paralinguistic signals of communication.

When Mrs. Gupta enters her daughter's mind, she sees scenes of her own life in India - the past she so meticulously tried to hide. In the mother's words, "There are the moments from my life that I had banished from memory. But like much that is banished, they didn't leave. They went underground. And now, somehow, my daughter is dreaming them" (*QD* 259).

The trauma of the mother's life as an orphan remain largely unspoken. Even in Mrs.Gupta's journals she does not tell much about her childhood. Living as an orphan in the slums, facing hunger and deprivation, the mother is saved by her talent of dream- telling: "It afforded me some protection in that place where orphans were used in cruel ways" (*QD* 257). While dreaming together, the mother and the daughter in *Queen of Dreams* briefly form such an interment unit-a cognitive dyad that engages in communication, or more accurately in the dreaming, that allows the mother to access her repressed past. This communication occurs almost exclusively in the realm of dreams, where the mother's consciousness cannot fully control the appearance of her memories and traumatic experiences.

Rakhi is fascinated by the gift of vision and ability to foresee and guide people through their fates. With a world in alarming transition, she is struggling to keep her footing withher family. She longs for something to bring her mother and herself closer as Rakhi also feels unaware from her mother's past in India and the dream world she inhabits. Rakhi finds solace in the discovery, burdened by her own painful secret after her mother's death, through her dream journals. The long-closed door to Rakhi's past is opened by the journalwritten by Rakhi's mother.

In an attempt to prevent her daughter from experiencing an inevitable split between her Indian and American identities, the mother in *Queen of Dreams* hides her past. She eventually realizes that her reticence causes her daughter to imagine her own ethnicity through the western perspective. Only after the mother dies in a car accident do Rakhi and her father discover the mother's confessional dream – journal in which she finally allows her family a glimpse of her real self, and this becomes a tragic reality. The mother assumes that the daughter will turn to her father to fill in the gaps in her narrative though she is seen to be writing in Bengali, providing little cultural background regarding her native country. Hence, the task of cultural transmission is finally redirected to the father. The father answers Rakhi's basic need cocerning ethnic belonging, mutuality, and continuity, thus helping her to reconstruct her identity by explaining Indian culture to his daughter through the stories of his own life.

Rakhi's assumptions about her mother's intentions prove to be accurate. In one of the final sections of her journal, the dream teller admits: "I was not a good mother to Rakhi. I loved her, but not fully. To love someone fully is to give up selfhood, and I could not risk that. She knew this. Perhaps that is why she constantly longed to understand who I am, to become who I am" (*QD* 297). So that she could maintain her powers as a dream-teller, the gap between the mother and daughter is indeed initiated and sustained by the mother. As a child, the mother was taken away from the slums to the caves of dream – tellers where she was taught to use her talent and this is discussed in the Journal. But, Mrs. Gupta rebels against the elders and elopes with a young man (Rakhi's father) whom she meets on a trip to Calcutta although dream- tellers are not supposed to fall in love.

It remains somewhat incomplete since the mother (Mrs.Gupta) cannot actively participate in the familial reconciliation. The reconstruction of the father-daughter bond is nevertheless initiated by the mother's journals. The daughter comes to terms with her mother's death and slowly rediscovers her father's unique character and talents as the father translates the journals to Rakhi, When the father and daughter start cooperating to save Rakhi's coffee shop, the daughter learns to trust her father and gradually relinquishes her anger, although at first Rakhi blames her father for her mother's death. The father and daughter realize that it is the first time they have spoken to each other directly without the mother's mediation. While sitting late into the night and sharing ideas:

"Through their excitement they are dimly aware that this is a first-ever event. Before this, all their interactions took place in the presence of the

mother, through her as it were. She was their conductor, their buffer

zone, their translator. She softened the combative edges of their words

and clarified their questions, even to themselves. I'll take care of it, she

whispered without words. Don't you worry?" (*QD* 165)

Rakhi indeed develops her relationship with both her mother and father. The mother's journals reveal secrets, providing the daughter the necessary context to understand her mother. On the other hand, her father's stories contribute comfort Rakhi's sense of alienation. When the father first tells her a story about India, the daughter: She leans forward, her eyes shining. Here is the kind of story she haswaited for her entire life, has begged, cajoled, badgered her mother for- in vain. And to think it was waiting all this time inside her father,the drinker, the singer, the skeptic who never believed in dreams. The parent she always dismissed, although affectionately, thinking he knew nothing she'd have any use for. (*QD* 168)

The subject that has the power to acknowledge another individual as an independent self, the relational identity Rakhi finally constructs allows her to reinterpret the ethnic other not as different, exotic or inexplicable. Rakhi succeeds in developing her unique painting style and starts creating authentic works of art that relate to her Indian – American experience after discarding the western, individualistic approach to herself.

Divakaruni establishes the theme of relationship among family members through a female protagonist from India. In the subtle, complex and traumatic process of becoming a new American, the readers witness a different woman. With the debilitating sense of loss, the novel portrays the exhilarating sense of possible clashes. Yet, the exuberant determination of the woman attracts the readers to them and denies the power of pity. Reflecting the American society, the novel *Queen of Dreams* competently reflects the trials and tribulations of an experience which can also be called as a trauma or pain. In this novel, Divakaruni has laid strong emphasis on the significance of familial ties, roots and self- rediscovery. Despite being an immigrant who faces all odds, the protagonist Rakhi in the novel has put in a lot of effort towards fighting the differences. She realizes and pays a lot of importance to relationships as she values them in the course . The novel depicts the successful journey that she undergoes and the way she holds the relationships together to rediscover her roots.

Rakhi's resilience of spirit and facing odds in life and accepting challenges creatively reflect the individualistic trait of the American life. She makes acculturation her strength, as towards the end of the novel she learns to appreciate that Indian instruments produce music that is not purely Indian but an American mix. She moves from there to a deeper philosophy of life which equips her to set right her estranged life with Sonny, her husband, in the dance hall "on the web of the world where Sonny and she have touched orbits once more" (*QD* 307), paving the way for an integrated family life, very much similar to that in an Indian setup. By adopting American ways, Rakhi moves towards success and stability in life, although temporarily she suffers a setback due to doubts about her sense of belonging and identity. She overcomes her challenges and rediscovers her identity.

It is interesting to see the unique relationship between an Indian born mother who is a dream- teller and her American born daughter who is a single mother, painter and a coffee shop owner. It is portrayed by Chitra Banerjee in her masterpiece *Queen of Dreams.* Rakhi is impressed by her mother Mrs. Gupta and feels that she does not have this inherited talent yet wishes for one. She finds it difficult to understand her mother's rituals which are mystical and unusual for her since childhood. When looked at the surface level, the relationship between the mother and the daughter seems to thrive on but the daughter is troubled by the feeling that she is continuously kept away from a part of her mother's life. It would not be true to say that the relationship between her mother and herself is put to risk because Rakhi is not able to comprehend dreams similar to her mother. Also, even after questioning repeatedly, her mother Mrs. Gupta refuses to tell anything about her life in India or makes any attempt to help her daughter Rakhi understand her native culture. This results in a complication when Rakhi makes a search for ethnic self-identity and through this she tries to imagine her home country as well her mother's life through western perspective of the majority culture.

Another twist in the plot happens when Rakhi makes attempts to reconstruct a sense of self by painting pictures that help her to come in terms with the unknown India through her art during bankruptcy. At the same time, she encounters a tragic and mysterious death of her mother in a car accident causing her mental trauma. However, the death of her mother opens up a new channel of communication between herself and her mother. The dream journals that Mrs. Gupta leaves behind reveal her past and the most intimate feelings about her life in the caves that she has always carried with her secretively. As the journals are written in Bengali, Rakhi finds it difficult to read and comprehend them without meditation. At this point she searches for help from her father Mr. Gupta. She requests him to translate the Bengali journals into English in order to know the content of it.

This establishes a bond between Rakhi and her father. Unlike her mother, her father feels very happy to talk about his past experiences in India to his daughter. On listening to the stories of her father and understanding the translation of the journals her father makes, Rakhi is seen to be reclaiming her ethnic self slowly. Also by working together with him, she manages to safeguard her business and transforms it into an authentic Indian snacks shop. She learns about her mother's supernatural ability and superhuman power to read other's minds and interpret dreams. On the other hand, Rakhi is ordinary with human cognition and therefore considers herself inferior and uninteresting. But it is to be noted that Rakhi has an ability to make clear assumptions of her mother's facial expressions, tone of voice and other paralinguistic signals but trivial. Even though Rakhi is successful in making assumptions and predictions based on her mother's facial expressions and bodily movements, when it comes to an exercise in dream telling, imitating her mother she becomes completely opaque to ordinary human understanding.

As her mind retreats to the realm of dreams, the body of her mother is found to be still. It is evident that, this state opposes her habitual perception of the world and Rakhi is frightened. Rakhi views her undecipherable mother as a total stranger, a mysterious mother since her natural communication capacities are so prone to reading minds.

For the first time, Rakhi also experiences herself as "separate, lesser being" (*QD* 162).

This feeling weaves a huge gap between the mother and the daughter throughout the novel. It is understood that not only the daughter but also the mother is having a weakness that, it is ironical on the part of the mother when she is able to read the minds of the strangers but incapable to comprehend the dreams of her own daughter and what they symbolize. When Rakhi is continuously disturbed by nightmares during her childhood, she runs to her mother for help. The mother also makes attempts to help her daughter understand the dream by entering into her dream and understand it by herself. When she does it, in the dream Rakhi is found standing in a lingerie section of a departmental store where a man would be found trying to seduce her through his words. Rakhi turns around and runs to him and they kiss. The mother fails to warn her daughter of the danger and later on could not interpret what the man in the dream symbolized, and when and where he would appear in her life again. Rakhi admires the dream telling ability of her mother and expects her to teach her how to interpret dreams. But she only is found spending her whole childhood failing to observe her mother in a vain attempt to relate to her. Later she figures out that her silent mother has an obstacle in their relationship. So she arrives at a conclusion that is, by acquiring the ability to tell dreams she would be able to communicate with her mother even without words and for which she urges to learn about her mother's past. When the mother enters her daughter's mind to witness her dreams, she witnesses scenes of her own life in India - the past she so meticulously tried to hide. Even in her journals she does not talk much about her childhood. The trauma of the mother's life as an orphan remains largely unspoken. Her mother is found deciding to keep distance from her child so that she can help people by practicing her dream telling power. The consequences of the same is faced by her when she understands that her daughter does not trust her and also she is haunted by the feeling that her mother's priorities are in the realm of ministry and not in her own family. On the contrary, it could be well understood that the assumptions that the daughter makes on her mother is not quite accurate. In one of the final sections of her journal, Mrs. Gupta herself states that she has not been a good mother to Rakhi. She has loved her, but not fully. She also emphasizes that to love someone fully is to give up selfhood, and that she could not risk it. Rakhi knows very well that her mother is never willing to give her selfhood up to be a dream interpreter and this is the reason why she constantly longed to understand who her mother was and wished to become a dream interpreter like her.

It is very evident from this that her mother Mrs. Gupta in order to practice and retain her boon- her power as a dream-teller keeps herself away from her daughter. While reading the journals, the daughter comes to know that her mother was taken from the slums into the caves of dream-tellers where she was kept to practice and bring out her talents. Also, it is prohibited for a dream-teller to fall in love but Rakhi's mother does it with the young man Mr. Gupta and elopes against the norms. After which the couple leaves to the United States where Rakhi's mother almost completely loses her dream-telling power for she shares her bed with her husband Mr. Gupta.

Not being able to dream further, Mrs. Gupta feels depressed and it is during this time a snake in the form of a the dream spirit comes to her in the dream. He tells her:

"Each time the dream teller had sex with her husband or even slept in the same bed, her power already weakened by being so far from the caves- dwindled further" (QD 314). She decides to "break off all ties with her husband" and return to the caves to regain her talent but to her shock, she discovers that she isconceived with Rakhi which makes it difficult for her to return to the caves to resume dream-telling.

The family malfunctions when the mother distances herself from her husband and daughter. Rakhi can be seen to be continuously longing for her mother's love and attention while the father in the family sinks to drinking habit. Rakhi's bonding with her father can also be considered as dysfunctional throughout her childhood. The strong love that the daughter has over her mother can be seen to be overshadowing every attempt the father makes to connect with his daughter. It can also be noted that despite the fact that her father is more accessible than her mother who is a mystery, she often disregards him preferring only the company of her mother. The dynamics in the family can be clearly understood by Rakhi's curious description of differences between her father and mother.

It is the mother-daughter bond that fascinates and makes Rakhi uneasy even though her father is easily accessible. Whereas for Mrs. Gupta, if she wishes to maintain her talent of dream- telling, the community of dream-tellers is the only intermental unit she can join with. In her journals the mother explains: When dream tellers live closer to one another, their threads combine to form a powerful rope that can bear the weight of even the most difficult dream...Dream tellers should not travel too far from their community, because they depend on each other for successful practice of their talent. (*QD* 311)

When considering the lifestyle of the dream-tellers, they are trained in an utterly relational and independent environment and it is understood that there is left only a very little space for individual desires and rebellion. Rakhi's mother is seen to be outstanding as she makes a choice to trouble and stand against this perfect harmony of minds in order to assert individuality. Attaining this independence has cost her more than she thought. She begins to feel lonely and even longs to return to the community because she is afraid of losing her power. It could be clearly understood that the journals she writes act as a bridge to reach her family and explain the truth about herself. It is after her death in a car accident, Rakhi experiences a close bonding with her father which helps her to understand the journal written by her mother in Bengali. The comprehension of the journal helps Rakhi to understand the state of her mother, the circumstances that caused her to have an intermental bond with her daughter. While reading the novel, it is noted that the mother refuses to encourage verbal communication with her family throughout the novel. She speaks very little but tries to mean a lot of things. In order to strengthen her dream-telling talent, her mother restrains herself from speaking much to her own family. Mrs. Gupta uses words only to instruct her daughter to speak with her clients as they are her precious commodity and uses them only when it is necessary. Story-telling is one such a thing that Rakhi always craves for but she does not get it as her mother would never tell her even a bedtime story but on the other hand would encourage her daughter to narrate one. Though stories have in many ways improved her daughters' imagination, they do not provide her with a sense of belonging or even identification of her mother or even her own ethnicity.

In a child's identity construction, the parents' storytelling about their past plays an important role. By actively participating in it and by engaging in their parents' stories, children are allowed to relate to their parents' culture. Conversational stories of personal experiences achieve face to face communication and the importance of it cannot be emphasized enough. An active participation in the story results in a way to make it more relevant to their personalities is achieved by listening to it. This kind of communication is in which the father and the daughter engage in during the story-telling time. A good effort is made by Rakhi to initiate an increase of her father's story telling interest where her father also looks to be very willing to narrate stories of his time in India. This indirectly brings about the faciliation of dialogic interaction with the daughter and thus helping her to direct his stories in a course which is more useful and relevant to her.

It is vivid that the mother fails to teach Rakhi how to engage in socio-cultural interactions and as a result it hampers the construction of her identity when her mother herself fails to engage in a mutual, social and preferably verbal relationship with her child. It could also be noted that the mother admits her mistake that she decided not to tell her daughter about India shortly before her death.

The mother re-establishes her authority over her daughter even after she becomes a grown up by explaining her motives while she notices her similarity in her child. She also emphasizes her best intentions and takes responsibility for her choices in raising her daughter. She makes her daughter feel an outsider both to her mother's past and her family's ethnic identity while she attempts to protect her daughter from feeling an outsider in America.

Her father helps his daughter tounderstand her ethnic identity while the mother merely identifies Rakhi's distorted self-identity. His talents as a chef and later as a singer make the Indian culture more substantial and accessible to Rakhi when histories provide her with the necessary cultural context to imagine India in a realistic way. He suggests that they transform her ordinary coffee shop into an authentic "Indian snack shop, a chaerdokan, as it would be called in Calcutta" (QD 185). While he helps his daughter to save the coffee shop, he initiates to make various authentic desserts using his experience as a helper in a snack shop during his adolescence in India. They together transform Rakhi's business into a standard Indian place as per her mother's advice. Yet, another problem they suffer from is that the insufficient attraction it gives to the customers who are continuously tempted by a competing coffee shop, which is affiliated with "the fastest growing cafe chain in the country".

The situation is managed by the father's singing. Her father makes it possible to attract the attention of a stranger who asks him whether he knows even other Hindi songs while humming to himself an Indian melody.

To the basic human need for emotional connection and artistic expression is how the association created by the musicians in Rakhi's coffee shop appeals Rakhi to revise her understanding of art and ethnic identity by participating in the musical, cosmopolitan ceremonies in her coffee shop. Looking at her own paintings she "feels detached from the work she did before, as if it were painted by someone else, and not someone she particularly admires. There's a static feel, particularly, to her paintings about India. As her mother would say, they're not authentic" (*QD* 220). Rakhi decides that she wants "to create something new, something different and magical," yet it is only when she comes across the work of other Indian painters that she is able to start re-conceptualizing her own art.

As interdependent components of Rakhi's self, art and identity can be shown. She is capable of breaking the binaries between what traditionally is seen as American or Indian when she absorbs the new ways of artistic expression that as Charles Taylor suggests "we become full human agents, capable of understanding ourselves, and hence of defining our identity, through our acquisition of rich human languages of expression" (79). Rakhi is provided with alternative ways of self-rediscovery by her mother's journals and her father's stories, as well as the band's cosmopolitan music and the Indian-American paintings. She realizes that there are more than one way to be ethnic or Indian-American through these meaningful exchanges with others. On a clear understanding, one is able to accept that Rakhi finally rediscovers her individuality as an independent self through her forage for her parental roots. Rakhi succeeds in developing her unique painting style and starts creating an authentic work of arts that relate to her Indian-American experience after discarding the western individualistic approach to herself. These meaningful changes in Rakhi depicts a successful journey from Shadows to Roots and the way she holds her relationships together to rediscover her self. Similar to this novel, Divakaruni has strongly penned the depiction of parental relationship, searching for their roots and finding them from the shadows.

The novel *Oleander Girl* is an amazing story of Korobi Roy who is the protagonist. The protagonist is given the identity as 'Roy' which she is ignorant of. Later as the story progresses, her grandmother unravels a mystery about her birth and her parentage which necessitates her to go on in search of her parents' past and family secret. Korobi is an eighteen years old orphan girl who is parented by her grandparents. The protagonist seems to long for the love of her parents a lot in her childhood days. The only thing she knows about her parents is that her mother Anu Roy died during parturition and her father in a car crash three months before her mother's death. Though the protagonist has a great desire to know more about her parents, she finds certain obstacles in it that she is supposed to be married to Rajat Bose who is from a rich Bengali family. It is on the day of her engagement, she learns more unbelievable truths about her parents. A shadow of her mother appears in her dreams and gives her some vague clues about her father but she feels hesitant to share it with her grandmother.

The truth about her parents completely ruins her peace of mind which she is exposed to by her grandmother Sarojini who unties the promise to her when her husband dies suddenly. The protagonist learns about her mother Anu from her grandmother that her mother was in love with a foreigner named Rob Lancey when she stayed in America for higher studies. She became pregnant from her premarital relationship with Rob Lancey and during her pregnancy she longed to be with her parents in India. She tried to convince her father to marry Rob but this ended in an unexpected argument and her father Bimal Roy, a retired conventional barrister finally denied it for it would mar the family reputation. Thus she could not decide her future.

After learning this long hidden secret, the protagonist makes a strong decision to leave for America in order to find her father and her identity. Finding her father in an unknown country just with the help of a photograph of her mother and his first name becomes very difficult for her. Yet she decides to talk to Rajat about her desire and her stern decision to find out her father. She is very much urged to take the challenge and explore the whereabouts of her father in the foreign land. Though she seemed to be interested to get married first and then go into the exploring her father,suddenly she ascertains not to get entangled into the marital life and puts her marriage plans aside. Korobi thus proves wilful, charismatic and is always prepared of people and their comments.

Karobi says, "I don't care!" (*OG* 71) though Rajat tries to persuade her explaining about the less possibilities in finding her father. She decides to give up her peaceful, satisfying and secured life in Kolkata and also the engagement with the elite class Rajat in order to find her father. She advances to choose the challenging path which is not a bed of roses. She thus ventures to America even after knowing the fact that all the adversities and misfortunes are on her way, like other immigrants. The protagonist Karobi journeys in search of her parental roots substantiating the words of Sri Aurobindo who says, a person is considered to be great when he is calm inspite of being alone. Without knowing her real identity and being alone in America Korobi goes through hard times. It is at Kennedy airport, the very first turbulence is encountered by Karobi. She is put to trouble when the person arranged by Rajat fails to receive her. More hardship follow her until she strives hard to find her father which ultimately tests her patience.

The protagonist learns from her father in America that, he visited India looking for his wife Anu Roy and the newborn but he was informed that both of them are dead by her in- laws. He also informs Karobi that he is married and has begotten three children. By hearing this, she gets very disturbed to think that she is an illegitimate child and the thought suffocates her. Duing her stay in America she gets attracted towards Vic who understands the crisis of Karobi and continues to support her throughout her endeavours. After realizing her status that her father is now someone else's husband and father, the protagonist is left to make a new choice. She says: "I'll have to make my new decision: Vic or Rajat, America or India" (*OG* 218). Faithfulness for her fiance and many other feelings about being Indian brings her back to India and apparently these are the values that she learnt from her grandparents. She returns from America as a refined person who is capable to decide what is right for her and knows to resist her temptations. From the web of identity crisis she finds the roots of her through her father and gets liberated herself from the inner urge and decides to be a beautiful oleander that her mother wanted her to be. A sense of fulfilment is achieved by Karobi. A different dimension to her life opens up by the new facts she has learnt in her life.

When the protagonist faces a setback in life, the courage and stubbornness she newly has acquired enables her to go ahead with life. She does not feel much disappointed when she is rejected by Rajat and his mother because of the new attire and attitude with which she returns from America. Instead, she only becomes strong enough to face them and returns the engagement ring with much dignity. When considering the protagonist's life in India, it could be said that she was put under strict conventions and overprotective life that she has to protect the family reputation, culture and tradition. She is not allowed to decide on her own but when circumstantial relationships force her, she makes a choice to find her real self and that leads her to venture a new world(America). The way Korobi takes the reality in her stride highlights her as a girl of mettle. Her broken engagement with Rajat or her newly found identity fails to curb Korobi's spirit for a new beginning. She is happy with Sarojini, her grandmother, in their old house; she starts her college again to keep herself busy. At the end she turns out to be a different Korobi who can understand the nuances of every relationship and handle them better than before. On the day of her wedding, she is a fully blown oleander - beautiful but tough and ready to take challenges. Thus at the end of the novel, we find that Korobi has grown into an individual woman by rediscovering her roots from shadows.

Bibliography

Divakaruni, Chitra Banerjee. *Oleander Girl.* New Delhi: Penguin Random House,
2013. Print.

... *Queen of Dreams*. Great Britain: Abacus, 2008. Print..
Great Britain: Abacus, 2008. Print.

Printed by Libri Plureos GmbH in Hamburg,
Germany